FASHION FIGURES

LAUREN CONRAD

CALIFORNIA COOL

LIFESTYLE DESIGNER

Jessica Rusick

Checkerboard
Library

An Imprint of Abdo Publishing
abdobooks.com

abdobooks.com

Published by Abdo Publishing, a division of ABDO, PO Box 398166, Minneapolis, Minnesota 55439.
Copyright © 2020 by Abdo Consulting Group, Inc. International copyrights reserved in all countries.
No part of this book may be reproduced in any form without written permission from the publisher.
Checkerboard Library™ is a trademark and logo of Abdo Publishing.

Printed in the United States of America, North Mankato, Minnesota
052019
092019

 THIS BOOK CONTAINS
RECYCLED MATERIALS

Design: Aruna Rangarajan, Mighty Media, Inc.
Production: Mighty Media, Inc.
Editor: Rachael L. Thomas
Design Elements: Shutterstock Images
Cover Photograph: Shutterstock Images
Interior Photographs: AP Images, pp. 15, 16-17, 21; Getty Images, pp. 19, 25; Seth Poppel/Yearbook
Library, p. 7; Shutterstock Images, pp. 5, 9, 11, 13, 23, 27, 28 (left, right), 29 (left, right)

Library of Congress Control Number: 2018966440

Publisher's Cataloging-in-Publication Data

Names: Rusick, Jessica, author.
Title: Lauren Conrad: California cool lifestyle designer / by Jessica Rusick
Other title: California cool lifestyle designer
Description: Minneapolis, Minnesota : Abdo Publishing, 2020 | Series: Fashion figures | Includes online
    resources and index.
Identifiers: ISBN 9781532119507 (lib. bdg.) | ISBN 9781532173967 (ebook)
Subjects: LCSH: Conrad, Lauren (Lauren Tell)--Juvenile literature. | Fashion designers--United States--
    Biography--Juvenile literature. | Television personalities--Biography--Juvenile literature. | Women authors,
    American--Biography--Juvenile literature. | Women entrepreneurs--Biography--Juvenile literature.
Classification: DDC 746.920922 [B]--dc23

CONTENTS

CALIFORNIA DREAMER

Californian Lauren Conrad is a reality TV star turned fashion designer. Her designs are inspired by her casual California **lifestyle**. Conrad's clothes often feature pastel colors and soft fabrics. She mixes **vintage** and modern styles to create simple, fashionable clothing for women of many shapes and sizes.

Today, Conrad runs the successful fashion line LC Lauren Conrad. Conrad also runs a **nonprofit** organization called The Little Market and a popular lifestyle **blog**.

Conrad starred on two reality TV shows when she was younger. But Conrad was never passionate about a career in television. She used her fame to break into the fashion industry. Her decision to forge her own path led to her becoming a modern-day fashion icon.

IN HER OWN WORDS

"It's really important to do things your own way."
—Lauren Conrad

By 2018, Lauren Conrad had more than 10 million social media followers.

EARLY FASHION FAN

Lauren Katherine Conrad was born on February 1, 1986, in Laguna Beach, California. She grew up in Laguna Beach with younger siblings Breanna and Brandon. Lauren's mother, Katherine, was a stay-at-home parent. Lauren's father, James, worked as an **architect**. James designed the Conrads' family home.

Lauren's father was not the only creative person she grew up around. She was also close with a neighbor who sometimes watched her after school. This neighbor was an artist. Being surrounded by creativity influenced Lauren's future career path.

From a young age, Lauren loved clothing. Growing up, she was often more interested in clothing than in schoolwork. It soon became Lauren's dream to one day design clothes. Her parents encouraged her creativity. As she grew older, Lauren developed her own special sense of style. She found she liked clothes that had a casual, beachy vibe.

Lauren (*left*) with her sister, Breanna

Lauren attended Laguna Beach High School in California. Her high school experience was not at all typical. During her senior year, she starred on a reality TV show. Though she didn't know it at the time, this experience would help Lauren become a fashion designer!

REALITY TV STAR

Conrad spent her late teenage years in front of a camera crew. At age 18, she starred in the reality show *Laguna Beach: The Real Orange County*. The show first aired on the TV network MTV in 2004. It features Conrad and her friends in their senior year at Laguna Beach High School.

Laguna Beach was a massive hit! Millions of people tuned in to follow the lives of Conrad and other wealthy, young students. By 2006, Conrad and *Laguna Beach* had become so popular that MTV decided to make another show. It was called *The Hills*.

In *The Hills*, viewers follow Conrad as she pursues a career in fashion. Each 30-minute episode features Conrad's work, life, and love interests. It soon became

FASHION FACT

Looking back on *Laguna Beach*, Conrad says her outfits were "head-to-toe bad."

Laguna Beach is well known for being a creative hub for artists.

MTV's highest-rated show! Millions of viewers became invested in Conrad's journey at college and beyond. The friends Conrad made as she explored the fashion industry even became cast members.

While starring in *The Hills*, Conrad first attended the Academy of Art University in San Francisco, California. After one semester, she transferred to the Fashion Institute of Design & Merchandising in Los Angeles, California, to study product development.

While studying, Conrad did an **internship** with the fashion magazine *Teen Vogue*. There, she helped with photoshoots and learned about the fashion industry. Conrad also interned at the fashion PR firm People's Revolution.

Filming *The Hills* was not always easy for Conrad. She didn't like that some scenes were made up for entertainment. During one season of *The Hills*, Conrad even had to pretend to be in love with somebody she had never met!

However, being on TV also provided Conrad with special opportunities. It allowed her to meet people and **market** herself. MTV arranged the internship at *Teen Vogue*. The network also helped pay for Conrad to begin designing her first fashion line. This would be Conrad's first real opportunity to design and produce her own clothes.

When Conrad left *The Hills*, she said she was ready to begin her "real life."

FIRST FASHION LINE

In 2007, Conrad launched The Lauren Conrad Collection. That same year, several department stores in Los Angeles agreed to sell her clothes.

Conrad's collection **debuted** at Los Angeles Fashion Week in 2008. But The Lauren Conrad Collection received poor reviews from both fashion critics and consumers. One critic said that Conrad's clothes were made with cheap-looking fabric. And many consumers felt that Conrad's clothing cost too much.

Department stores stopped selling Conrad's clothing later that year. In 2009, Conrad stopped making clothing for The Lauren Conrad Collection. She also left *The Hills*.

Conrad was nervous to leave the reality show. But she wanted to focus all her energy on clothing design. Conrad wanted to prove that she could learn from her mistakes. It was time to become a full-time fashion designer.

In 2009, Conrad published her first book, *L. A. Candy*. The book was a *New York Times* best seller!

KOHL'S COMEBACK

Conrad did not let the failure of her first fashion line stop her from designing clothes. In 2009, she partnered with the department store Kohl's to design and launch a brand-new fashion line, LC Lauren Conrad.

Working with Kohl's, Conrad learned how to design with economics in mind. To earn a profit, Conrad had to sell her clothes for more money than it cost to make them. If she made her clothes with expensive fabric, she would have to charge her customers high prices. But Conrad had learned that consumers did not want to buy her clothing if it was too expensive. So, Conrad learned to find fabrics that look stylish and high quality but are low cost.

Conrad also faced another design challenge at Kohl's. She wanted to design **chiffon** tops for her fashion line. But Kohl's sales staff said its customers would not buy chiffon tops, because the fabric is see-through.

WEST COAST WEAR

The look and feel of LC Lauren Conrad draws from Conrad's West Coast **lifestyle**. Conrad likes casual clothes that can be dressed up or dressed down. She also likes pastel colors and soft, sheer, flowing fabrics.

Though she lives in California, Conrad's clothes are designed at Kohl's offices in New York. Each month, Conrad flies to New York to design and approve her line's new pieces.

Conrad thought that customers would like **chiffon** tops if they knew how to style them. She came up with the idea to put tags on the shirts showing her personal styling advice. Customers responded positively to the advice, and the tops were a success!

The chiffon tops were not the only successful LC Lauren Conrad item. The entire line was a hit! Conrad enjoyed working with Kohl's to develop her line. But with Kohl's as a partner, Conrad could not make the final decisions on her clothing. Conrad decided she wanted to be in charge of her own fashion line.

Conrad has said she wants her products to help everyone feel effortlessly fashionable.

PAPER CROWN

In 2010, Conrad founded the clothing line Paper Crown with her friend Maura McManus. Paper Crown drew from Conrad's **signature** style, but was edgier than LC Lauren Conrad. Conrad also used more expensive fabrics for Paper Crown, like silk.

Conrad's work at Paper Crown was very different from her work with the LC Lauren Conrad line. Conrad handled all of Paper Crown's creative decisions. This included sketching fashion designs and picking out different fabrics to compare.

The team working at Paper Crown was also much smaller than that for LC Lauren Conrad. Usually there were only three people in Paper Crown's office!

IN HER OWN WORDS

"I've transformed past mistakes into flourishing brands and businesses. As basic as it may sound, learning from your mistakes is a vital part of becoming a successful **entrepreneur.**"
—Conrad

Conrad with
Paper Crown
co-founder
Maura McManus

Conrad and McManus worked to make a detailed plan for the launch of Paper Crown. Before starting the company, the pair carefully studied other clothing companies. They wanted to understand how these companies made, sold, and **marketed** their clothes.

Conrad and McManus also created a plan for promoting their company to buyers. Conrad used social media to spread the word about Paper Crown. She also appeared on the cover of *Lucky* magazine with her Paper Crown designs. The magazine cover sparked interest from stores such as Nordstrom. In 2011, Nordstrom was one of the first to sell Paper Crown clothes.

The Paper Crown brand became a success! But Conrad wanted to do more. She wanted to use her fashion knowledge to help others, save the planet, and support women.

FASHION FACT

The name *Paper Crown* was inspired by Conrad's days playing dress-up at her grandma's house. Conrad would make paper crowns to wear with her dress-up clothes.

The boutique store CUSP promoted Paper Crown in November 2011.

MAKING A DIFFERENCE

Conrad had become a well-known fashion figure. She wanted to use her design skills to affect positive change. In 2012, Conrad partnered with the company BlueAvocado. BlueAvocado works to create **eco-friendly** product designs.

Together, BlueAvocado and Conrad created bags for makeup, shopping, and travel. The bags were made from a material called Repreve. One bag made from Repreve was created from up to seven recycled water bottles!

The following year, Conrad visited the Indonesian island Bali with friend Hannah Skvarla. During the trip, the friends

FASHION FACT

In 2013, Conrad won an UnBottle the World Award. The company SodaStream gives this award to those who help the **environment**.

Markets in Bali showcase the island's traditional culture. Tourists can buy locally made textiles, crafts, and art.

visited a local market. They met local women who were selling handmade items to support their families.

Meeting the women inspired Conrad and Skvarla to launch a charitable project called The Little Market in October 2013. The Little Market website helps women **entrepreneurs** sell items they make. By 2018, The Little Market helped more than 50 artists to connect with customers all over the world!

FASHION & LIFESTYLE ICON

Conrad's many projects have made her a fashion and **lifestyle** expert. In 2011, Conrad began documenting her experiences on her personal website, laurenconrad.com. Over time, it has become a place for fans to gather and learn from her.

On her website, Conrad wrote regularly about fashion, beauty, fitness, and home decorating. And while Conrad's career was growing, her family was as well. In 2014, Conrad married musician William Tell. In 2017, they had a son, Liam.

IN HER OWN WORDS

"The best brands are like no other. The ones that really stand apart are organic and true, so I was never looking to be the next anyone."
—Conrad

Conrad often talked about being a mom on her **blog**. She shared updates and fun facts about her personal life as a wife, mother, and **entrepreneur**. She also gave advice to readers with life questions.

Conrad and her husband, William Tell,
married in 2014 at a winery in Santa
Ynez Valley, California.

LAUREN CONRAD TODAY

Conrad's fashion projects continue to grow and evolve. In September 2018, her **nonprofit** organization The Little Market opened its first store in Los Angeles. Meanwhile, the LC Lauren Conrad line expanded to include swimwear, shoes, sunglasses, and more.

In 2018, Conrad **debuted** her LC Lauren Conrad Weekend Collection. The collection was inspired by Conrad becoming a mom. She wanted to design weekend looks that were both stylish and comfortable. Next, Conrad wants to design children's clothes.

In August 2018, MTV announced that it was making a new season of *The Hills*. Conrad will not join the cast. She is too busy growing her fashion empire!

Conrad's elegant style shines through all her projects. She pushed past her early setbacks and built a brand that reflects her life and passions. She is a fashion success story.

"Television was just sort of an accident...I never felt really strongly about it. But fashion is something I feel passionate about."
—*Conrad in a 2015 interview with* Cosmopolitan *magazine*

TIMELINE

Conrad launches The Lauren Conrad Collection, her first fashion line.

Conrad partners with Kohl's to launch LC Lauren Conrad.

Laguna Beach premieres on MTV.

2004

2007

2009

1986

2006–2009

2008

Conrad stars on *The Hills*.

Lauren Katherine Conrad is born on February 1 in Laguna Beach, California.

The Lauren Conrad Collection debuts at Los Angeles Fashion Week to mixed reviews.

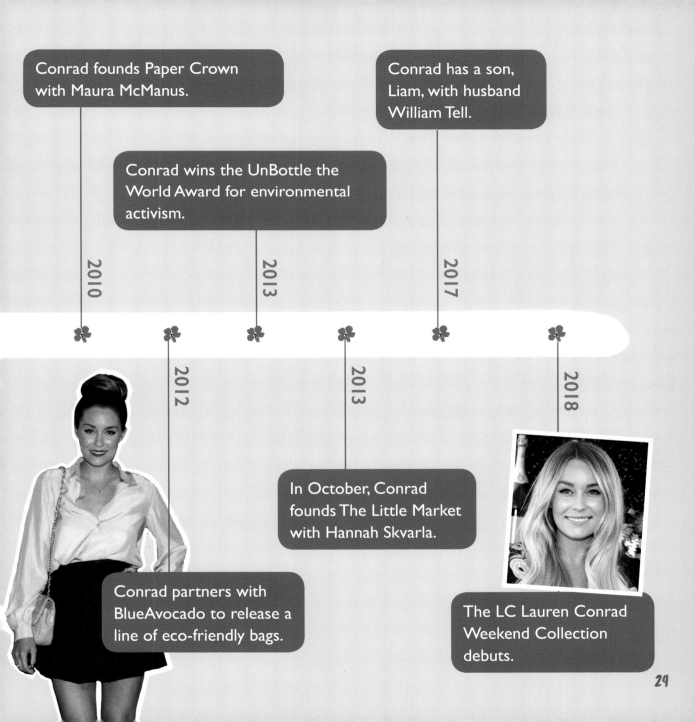

Conrad founds Paper Crown with Maura McManus.

Conrad wins the UnBottle the World Award for environmental activism.

Conrad has a son, Liam, with husband William Tell.

2010

2013

2017

2012

2013

2018

Conrad partners with BlueAvocado to release a line of eco-friendly bags.

In October, Conrad founds The Little Market with Hannah Skvarla.

The LC Lauren Conrad Weekend Collection debuts.

GLOSSARY

architect (AHR-kuh-tehkt)—a person who plans and designs buildings.

blog—an online story that tells about someone's personal opinions, activities, and experiences. A person who writes a blog is a blogger.

chiffon—a flowing, sheer fabric, often made of silk.

debut—to present or perform something for the first time.

eco-friendly—not causing harm to the environment.

entrepreneur—one who organizes, manages, and accepts the risks of a business or an enterprise.

environment—nature and everything in it, such as the land, sea, and air.

internship—guided practical experience in a professional field. A person doing an internship is called an intern.

lifestyle—the way a being, group, or society lives.

market—to advertise or promote an item for sale. This process is called marketing.

nonprofit—not existing or carried on for the purpose of making a profit.

signature—something that sets apart or identifies an individual, group, or company.

vintage—old but still interesting or of good quality.

ONLINE RESOURCES

To learn more about Lauren Conrad, please visit **abdobooklinks.com** or scan this QR code. These links are routinely monitored and updated to provide the most current information available.

INDEX